Let's-Read-and-Find-Out Science®

DINOSAUR BONES

by ALIKI

HarperCollins*Publishers*

for Bruce Leonard, Marie, Peter, Eve and Philip

With special thanks to Franklyn Branley, who started my interest in dinosaurs,
and Pam Hastings, for her patience and help on this book.

The *Let's-Read-and-Find-Out Science* book series was originated by Dr. Franklyn M. Branley, Astronomer Emeritus and former Chairman of the American Museum–Hayden Planetarium, and was formerly co-edited by him and Dr. Roma Gans, Professor Emeritus of Childhood Education, Teachers College, Columbia University. Text and illustrations for each of the books in the series are checked for accuracy by an expert in the relevant field. For more information about Let's-Read-and-Find-Out Science books, write to HarperCollins Children's Books, 10 East 53rd Street, New York, NY 10022.

Library of Congress Cataloging-in-Publication Data
Aliki.
   Dinosaur bones.
   (Let's-read-and-find-out science. Stage 2)
   Summary: Discusses how scientists, studying fossil remains, provide information on how dinosaurs lived millions of years ago.
   1. Dinosaurs—Juvenile literature. [1. Dinosaurs. 2. Fossils]
I. Title. II. Series.
QE862.D5A3425   1988   567.9′1   85-48246
ISBN 0-690-04549-2
ISBN 0-690-04550-6 (lib. bdg.)
ISBN 0-06-445077-5 (pbk.)

DINOSAUR BONES

The first time anyone ever mentioned
a giant fossil bone was in 1676.
The Reverend Dr. Robert Plot drew it
and described it as a "human thigh bone."

It turned out to be a dinosaur bone.

The first dinosaur I ever saw was in a book.
There were pictures of all different kinds.
The book said what dinosaurs ate and where they lived.
It said they all died out 65 million years ago.

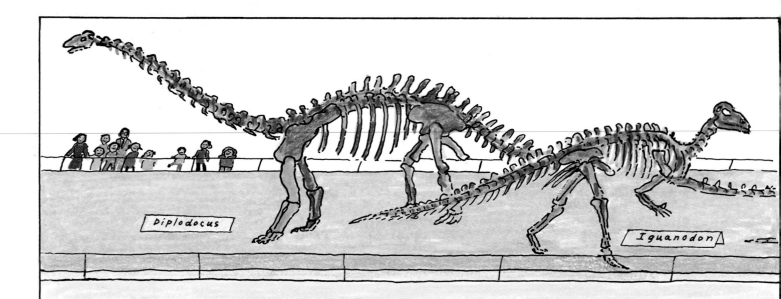

Then I went to the museum and saw dinosaur bones.
The pictures in the book seemed to come alive.
I could see how big dinosaurs really were.
I was glad the skeletons didn't move.

I wondered how people know so much about dinosaurs.
How do they know what dinosaurs looked like
  if they never saw one?
How do they know dinosaurs ever existed?

Tyrannosaurus

For a long time, people didn't know.

Then they began to find fossils.

Fossils are the remains of animals and plants
   that died long ago.

The animals and plants were preserved in mud or sand
   and slowly turned to stone.

People found fossil shells, leaves, and fish.

They found fossils of creatures that no longer exist.

The fossils were clues to the distant past,

   long before human beings appeared on earth.

The more fossils people found,

   the more curious they became.

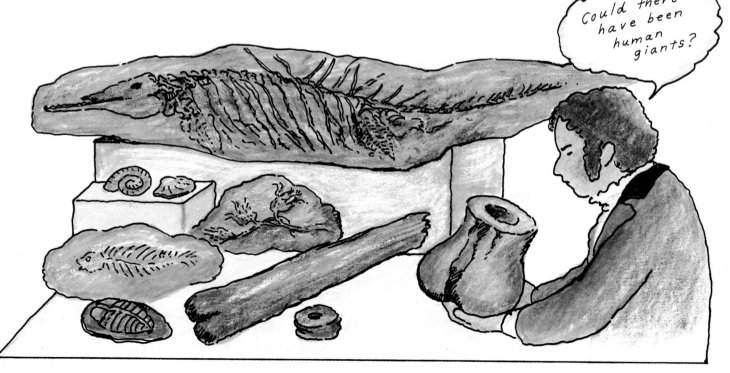

Mrs. Mantell didn't know it, but she found the first fossil that scientists would identify as part of a dinosaur.

In 1822, in England, Mary Ann Mantell spotted some
strange, giant fossil teeth in a pile of rocks near a quarry.
She showed them to her husband, a doctor who
collected fossils.
Dr. Gideon Mantell had never seen such teeth.
What an exciting find!
He searched the quarry.
He found a few more teeth and some bones.
What giant did they belong to?
No one knew.

Dr. Mantell had his ideas and wrote them down.

He said the teeth and bones belonged to a giant, plant-eating
   reptile that lived during the Mesozoic era, millions of years ago.

He could tell its age from the rock the teeth and bones
   were buried in.

He drew the animal as he thought it looked.

He named it Iguanodon, which means iguana tooth.

Dr. Mantell gave Iguanodon its name
when he discovered the fossil teeth were
like the teeth of the iguana lizard.

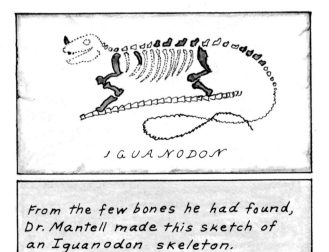

IGUANODON

From the few bones he had found,
Dr. Mantell made this sketch of
an Iguanodon skeleton.

Scientists laughed.

A giant reptile! Millions of years old!

But Dr. Mantell was convinced.

He searched on, hoping to find more bones.

Then he would have better proof.

Meanwhile, people uncovered more giant fossils.

Scientists studied the finds, piece by piece.

They wrote about them.

They exchanged ideas and information.

The teeth are razor sharp — a giant meat eater's.

1824

In England, William Buckland described some bones and teeth that had been found.
He said they belonged to a giant reptile, which he named Megalosaurus.

These are bones of an armored reptile — very different from Iguanodon.

1832 Dr. Mantell described the skeleton of a giant reptile he named Hylaeosaurus.

1834 At last, Dr. Mantell found his dream — a mass of Iguanodon bones.

Bit by bit, Dr. Mantell was proved right.
All these fossils were indeed the remains
of a group of giant prehistoric reptiles.
Dr. Richard Owen named the group Dinosauria—
"terrible lizards."

These look like bird tracks—but what a bird!

1835 In America, Edward Hitchcock studied footprints that had been found in 1802. He mistakenly thought they were bird tracks.

We now know of nine such giant reptiles.

1841 Dr. Owen named the dinosaurs at a meeting of scientists.

After that, there was a blaze of interest.

An exhibition was held of life-sized dinosaur models.

The excited public flocked to see them.

Scientists celebrated the event.

1853 Waterhouse Hawkins worked closely with Dr. Owen to construct dinosaurs for the famous exhibition at Crystal Palace in London. Scientists held a banquet inside an unfinished model of Iguanodon.

People knew there must be more dinosaur bones,
  and there were.
Fossil hunters uncovered hundreds of fossils.
They found big ones and small ones and
  newly hatched babies.
They dug fossils out of cliffs and quarries,
  coal mines and riverbanks, all over the world.
Scientists pieced the bones together and gave
  each new dinosaur a name.

1878 More than thirty Iguanodon skeletons were found in a coal pit in Belgium. It took three years to dig them out.

Othniel Charles Marsh

Edward Drinker Cope

Meanwhile, two American professors spent years in a race to collect more than the other. Between them, they found 136 new dinosaurs.

Early ideas changed.

Early mistakes were corrected.

1853   The Iguanodon modeled by
Waterhouse Hawkins had a horn
on its nose.

After the find in Belgium in 1878,
scientists knew the horn was
really a thumb.

1914 A sketch of Anatosaurus by
Arthur Lakes had a flexible tail.

Later, scientists discovered the
tail was thick and powerful.

With every find, scientists learned more and more
about dinosaurs and their world.

1854 With just a few bones to go by,
Dr. Owen thought Megalosaurus
walked on four legs.

Later, scientists discovered
it walked on two legs.

O.giganteus

O. tuberosus

C. ingens

1835 - 1864
    Edward Hitchcock spent 30 years
    collecting and describing tracks,
    and made careful drawings of them.
    He died thinking they were made
    by giant prehistoric birds.

    Later, scientists realized they
    were dinosaur tracks.

The earth looked different then.

It was not separated into many continents, as it is today.

It was just one mass of land, surrounded by water.

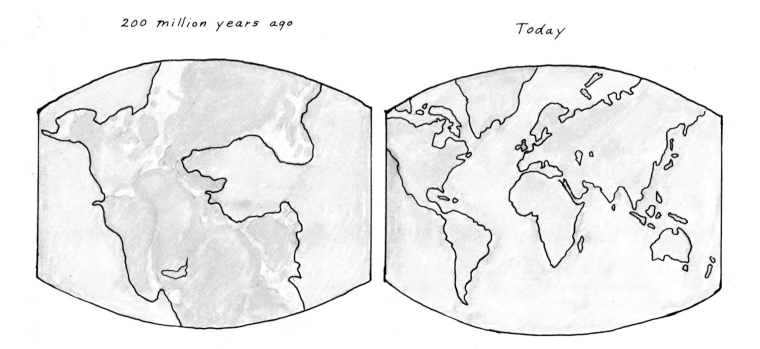

200 million years ago

Today

Dinosaurs could roam freely all over the world.

There weren't many high mountains or oceans to stop them.

The weather was warm everywhere—
   perfect for dinosaurs to thrive in.

And they did thrive—for 140 million years.

How do we know?

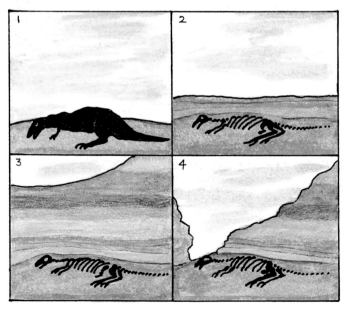

From fossils, that's how we know.

Fossils are found in rock layers, or strata.

The rock was once mud or sand.

Some dinosaurs were preserved in the mud.

They became fossils.

This is how it happened.

Long ago a dinosaur died.

Mud covered the dinosaur layer upon layer.

Slowly both the dinosaur and the mud
   turned to stone.

In time, more and more rock layers built up.

The rock in each layer is different.

Each layer contains its own fossils.

That is how scientists tell time.

CRETACEOUS PERIOD 135-65 million years ago

JURASSIC PERIOD 190-135 million years ago

TRIASSIC PERIOD 225-190 million years ago

MESOZOIC ERA 225-65 million years ago

Scientists divide time on earth into eras, and eras into periods.

Dinosaurs lived during three periods of the Mesozoic era.

We know that because their fossils were found only in those layers.

In that long Mesozoic time, dinosaurs changed and developed—
    they evolved.

Dinosaurs first appeared late in the Triassic period.

There weren't many.

They were mostly small.

Coelophysis

Procompsognathus

Plateosaurus

Heterodontosaurus

25

Then bigger dinosaurs evolved and multiplied.
During the Jurassic period, many grew to huge sizes.
The giant plant eaters—or herbivores—
  were the biggest dinosaurs ever.
There were big meat eaters—or carnivores—too.

Megalosaurus

Brachiosaurus

Diplodocus

Compsognathus

Ornitholestes

Apatosaurus

Stegosaurus

Allosaurus

Hylaeosaurus

Iguanodon

Corythosaurus

Hypsilophodon

By the Cretaceous period, dinosaurs had taken over.

There were crested ones, horned ones, and armored ones.

And there was the fierce king of them all, Tyrannosaurus rex.

The dinosaurs flourished.

It was their world.

Anatosaurus

Ankylosaurus

Pachycephalosaurus

Triceratops

Tyrannosaurus

Then suddenly, they all died out.
No one knows why.

There are many things we don't know about dinosaurs.
We wonder what colors they were,
    what noises they made.
We wonder if they were warm-blooded or cold-blooded.
Scientists search for more answers.
And I check in at the museum and read my new books
    for the latest news.

DINOSAURS IN THIS BOOK	PAGE	WHERE THEY WERE FOUND	WHEN THEY LIVED
ALLOSAURUS ("other lizard")	27	North America, Africa, Australia, Asia(?)	Late Jurassic
ANATOSAURUS ("harmless lizard")	18	Eastern North America	Late Cretaceous
ANKYLOSAURUS ("fused lizard")	29	North America (Montana and Canada)	Late Cretaceous
APATOSAURUS ("deceptive lizard")	26-27	Western U.S.A.	Late Triassic
BRACHIOSAURUS ("arm lizard")	26	U.S.A., East Africa	Late Jurassic
COELOPHYSIS ("hollow form")	24	Southwestern and Eastern U.S.A.	Late Triassic
COMPSOGNATHUS ("pretty jaws")	26	Germany	Late Jurassic
CORYTHOSAURUS ("helmet lizard")	28	Canada	Late Cretaceous
DIPLODOCUS ("double beam")	6, 26	U.S.A. (Colorado, Montana, Utah, Wyoming)	Late Jurassic
HETERODONTOSAURUS ("different-teeth lizard")	25	South Africa	Late Triassic
HYLAEOSAURUS ("woodland lizard")	14, 28	South West England	Early Cretaceous
HYPSILOPHODON ("high-ridge tooth")	28	England (Isle of Wight)	Early Cretaceous
IGUANODON ("iguana tooth")	6-7, 12, 15, 16, 17, 18, 28	Southern England, Belgium, North Africa, Romania, Western North America, Mongolia	Early Cretaceous
MEGALOSAURUS ("great lizard")	14, 19, 26	British Isles	Jurassic-Early Cretaceous
ORNITHOLESTES ("bird robber")	27	U.S.A. (Wyoming)	Late Jurassic
PACHYCEPHALOSAURUS ("thick-headed lizard")	29	Western U.S.A.	Late Cretaceous
PLATEOSAURUS ("flat lizard")	25	Europe (France, Germany, Switzerland)	Late Triassic
PROCOMPSOGNATHUS ("before Compsognathus")	24	Southwestern Germany	Late Triassic
STEGOSAURUS ("roofed lizard")	27	U.S.A. (Colorado, Oklahoma, Utah, Wyoming)	Late Jurassic
TRICERATOPS ("three-horned face")	29	Western North America	Late Cretaceous
TYRANNOSAURUS ("tyrant lizard")	7, 29	Western North America, China	Late Cretaceous

The dinosaurs in the scenes on pages 24 to 29 lived in different parts of the world. They did not necessarily live together as shown.